Giving up United States Citizenship

Arthur Crandon LL.B. (Hons.) M.A.

Giving up United States citizenship

Copyright Arthur Crandon 2024

All rights reserved. No part of this book may be reproduced, stored in a retrieval system, or transmitted in any form or by any means—electronic, mechanical, photocopying, recording, or otherwise—without the prior written permission of the publisher, except for brief quotations in critical reviews or articles.

This is a work of fiction. Names, characters, places, and incidents are either the product of the author's imagination or used fictitiously. Any resemblance to actual persons, living or dead, events, or locales is entirely coincidental

ISBN: 9798340774088

Cover design by Lynnie Ceniza
Interior design and formatting by Lynnie Ceniza
Published by Arthur Crandon Publishing
Visit our website: Arthurcrandon.co.uk

DISCLAIMER

The information provided in this book is for general informational purposes only. It does not constitute legal, financial, or professional advice. While every effort has been made to ensure accuracy, the author and publisher assume no responsibility for errors or omissions. Readers should consult with appropriate professionals for specific advice tailored to their individual circumstances.

First Edition: August 2024

Giving up your U.S. Citizenship is a difficult and long process and is not to be taken lightly..

CONTENTS

	Acknowledgments	i
1	Summary	1
2	The Benefits	7
3	The Downside	11
4	Statistics	15
5	Finding a new country	21
6	Reasons to Renounce	25
7	Exceptions to paying tax	27

There are advantages and disadvantages to renouncing your U.S. Citizenship. You should carefully consider your options, and take advice, before you proceed.

1 SUMMARY

Renouncing U.S. citizenship is a significant decision, and it's essential to understand the process thoroughly. Here's a step-by-step guide to help you navigate the path:

1. Renouncing U.S. citizenship is a significant decision, and understanding its implications is crucial. Let's delve into the details:

2. Renouncing U.S. Citizenship: Consequences and Considerations

Tax Implications:

3. The U.S. is one of the few countries that taxes its citizens on global income. If you renounce your U.S. citizenship, you may be

subject to the U.S. Exit Tax if you meet certain criteria. Essentially, this treats you as if you sold all your assets the day before expatriation.

4. Relief from U.S. taxes might be a benefit for those who no longer maintain significant ties with the U.S.

Loss of Rights and Privileges:

5. By renouncing U.S. citizenship, you relinquish several rights and privileges:
6. Voting: You won't be able to vote in U.S. federal, state, or local elections.
7. Residency and Work: You lose the right to live and work in the U.S. without a visa.
8. Constitutional Protections: You won't be protected by the U.S. Constitution.
9. U.S. Passport: You'll no longer have a U.S. passport, but you'll need one from another country for international travel.

Potential Bar to Re-entry:

10. Depending on your circumstances, renouncing citizenship might make it challenging to obtain visas to visit the U.S. in the future. In some cases, you could be barred from returning.

Cost and Legal Process:

11. There's a significant fee associated with the renunciation process.
12. You might also incur additional legal or professional fees to ensure the process is handled correctly.

Benefits of Renouncing U.S. Citizenship:

13. Relief from U.S. Taxes: If you no longer maintain significant ties with the U.S., you might no longer be subject to U.S. taxation on your worldwide income.
14. Simplification of Finances: Without the need to consider U.S. tax laws, financial planning might become more straightforward.
15. Political or Personal Reasons: Some individuals feel a stronger connection to another country or disagree with U.S. policies, making renunciation a symbolic act of separation.
16. Global Mobility: Renouncing U.S. citizenship might open up easier travel or residency opportunities in other parts of the world.

17. Remember that this decision is deeply

personal, and seeking professional advice is crucial. Consult with experts to make an informed choice tailored to your individual circumstances

Obtain a Second Passport:

- To renounce your U.S. citizenship, you'll need a second passport from another country. Obtain this passport before proceeding further.

Review the Renunciation Forms:
- Familiarize yourself with the necessary forms. The most critical form is the **DS-4079**, which is the "Request for Determination of Possible Loss of United States Citizenship." Prepare this form accurately.

Book Your Renunciation Appointment:
- Contact the nearest U.S. Embassy or Consulate to schedule an appointment for renunciation. The exact procedure may vary between different embassies or consulates.

Attend Your Renunciation Appointment:

- On the appointed day, appear in person before a U.S. consular or diplomatic officer at the U.S. Embassy or Consulate in a foreign country.
- Bring your second passport, the completed DS-4079 form, and any other required documents.
- You'll sign an oath of renunciation, officially relinquishing your U.S. citizenship.

File Your Final U.S. Tax Return:
- Before or after your renunciation appointment, ensure you've filed your final U.S. tax return. This includes reporting all income and fulfilling any tax obligations.
- Seek professional tax advice to ensure compliance with tax laws.

Receive the Certificate of Loss of Nationality (CLN):
- After completing the process, you'll receive a Certificate of Loss of Nationality (CLN). Keep this document safe, as it serves as proof of your renunciation.

Remember that each U.S. Embassy or Consulate may have specific requirements, so check their official website or contact them directly for precise instructions. Additionally, consider seeking legal advice to navigate the process smoothly.

2 THE BENEFITS

Renouncing U.S. citizenship is a significant decision, and it's essential to weigh the pros and cons carefully. While there are valid reasons for keeping U.S. citizenship, there are also benefits to giving it up. Here's a detailed list of the advantages of renouncing U.S. citizenship:

1. **Tax Relief**:
    - By renouncing U.S. citizenship, you escape the worldwide tax net. You'll no longer be subject to U.S. taxes on your global income. This can significantly reduce your income tax burden.
    - You won't need to file U.S. tax returns or report foreign financial accounts.
2. **Simplified Investment Planning**:

- Investment planning becomes more straightforward. You can plan to earn capital gains and interest income without worrying about U.S. taxation.
- Some U.S. tax rules won't apply to you anymore, simplifying your financial decisions.

3. **Avoiding Tax Changes**:
    - Changes to U.S. tax laws will no longer directly affect you. You'll be insulated from future tax policy shifts for expats.
    - This stability can be beneficial for long-term financial planning.

4. **Reduced Cross-Border Planning Costs**:
    - Managing finances across borders can be complex and costly. Renouncing U.S. citizenship eliminates the need for extensive cross-border tax planning.
    - You won't need to navigate dual tax systems or comply with U.S. reporting requirements.

5. **Freedom of Movement**:
    o Without U.S. citizenship, you won't be tied to U.S. residency requirements. You can live and work anywhere in the world without restrictions.
    o You'll have the flexibility to choose your ideal location based on personal preferences, career opportunities, or lifestyle.

6. **No Restrictions on US Travel**:
    o Contrary to common misconceptions, renouncing U.S. citizenship doesn't automatically prevent you from visiting the U.S. You can still travel there as a foreign national.
    o You'll enter the U.S. using a visa or the Visa Waiver Program (ESTA), just like any other non-U.S. citizen.

7. **Focus on Personal Goals**:
    o Renouncing citizenship allows you to prioritize personal goals over national ties. Whether it's building a global business, pursuing adventure, or embracing a different culture, you'll have more freedom to shape your life.

Remember that renouncing U.S. citizenship is a serious decision. It's essential to seek professional advice and consider your individual circumstances, goals, and emotional attachments. If you decide to proceed, ensure you follow the proper legal process.

3 THE DOWNSIDE

While there are valid reasons for keeping U.S. citizenship, there are also downsides to giving it up. Here's a detailed list of the disadvantages of renouncing U.S. citizenship:

1. **Loss of Rights and Privileges**:

    - By renouncing U.S. citizenship, you lose several rights and privileges:
        - **Right to Live and Work in the U.S.**: You'll no longer have the right to reside and work in the U.S. without immigration restrictions.
        - **Voting Rights**: You won't be able to vote in U.S. federal, state, or local elections.
        - **Protection from U.S.

Diplomatic Services: As a non-citizen, you won't have access to U.S. embassies or consulates for assistance while abroad.

2. **Expatriation Tax (U.S. Exit Tax)**:

   o When you renounce U.S. citizenship, you may be subject to an expatriation tax. This tax treats you as if you sold all your assets the day before expatriation, potentially resulting in significant tax liabilities.
   o The exit tax can apply to high-net-worth individuals or those with substantial assets.

3. **Difficulty in Reentering the U.S.**:

   o Depending on your circumstances, renouncing citizenship might make it challenging to obtain visas to visit the U.S. in the future.
   o You could face additional scrutiny when applying for U.S. visas.

4. **Emotional and Cultural Ties**:

    - Renouncing citizenship can be emotionally difficult, especially if you have strong cultural or familial ties to the U.S.
    - You may miss the sense of familiarity and identity associated with being a U.S. citizen.

5. **Statelessness Risk**:

    - If you renounce U.S. citizenship without having another citizenship, you could end up in a "stateless" status.
    - Statelessness can create practical challenges, including limited travel options and legal rights.

6. **Complex Legal Process**:

    - Renouncing citizenship involves paperwork, interviews, and legal procedures. It's not a simple or quick process.
    - Seek professional advice to ensure compliance with all requirements.

Remember that renouncing U.S. citizenship is a serious decision. It's essential to seek professional advice and consider your individual circumstances, goals, and emotional attachments. If you decide to proceed, ensure you follow the proper legal process.

4 STATISTICS

The number of people renouncing U.S. citizenship has been on the rise in recent years. Here are some relevant statistics:

1. **Annual Renunciations**:

    - Between **three thousand and six thousand** U.S. citizens have relinquished their citizenship each year since **2013**.
    - In **2020**, a record-breaking **10,000** people are estimated to have renounced U.S. citizenship.

2. **Reasons for Renunciation**:

    o The trend is not directly attributable to any particular election result or the COVID-19 pandemic.
    o Most Americans giving up their U.S. passport already live abroad and hold another citizenship.
    o The primary reasons cited include the burden of American anti-money laundering and counter-terrorism regulations, which make it onerous and expensive to maintain U.S. citizenship

The decision to renounce U.S. citizenship is significant, but it's not always irreversible. While most people who renounce their U.S. citizenship do so with the intention of permanently giving it up, there are situations where individuals seek to regain their citizenship. Here are some key points:

1. **Restoration of U.S. Citizenship**:

    o In certain cases, individuals who have lost their U.S. citizenship (whether through renunciation or other reasons) can seek to restore it.

- Restoration is more feasible if the loss of citizenship occurred while the person was a minor.

2. **Challenging the Loss of Citizenship**:

    - If you believe that your renunciation was done under duress or due to a psychological condition that inhibited decision-making, you can challenge the loss of citizenship.
    - This can be done through an administrative proceeding with the U.S. Department of State or by filing a lawsuit in a United States District Court.

3. **Complex Process**:

    - Seeking reinstatement of citizenship through a lawsuit can be expensive and procedurally difficult.
    - The State Department's administrative procedure is relatively informal, but consulting with an attorney knowledgeable in this area of law is advisable.

4. **State Department Discretion**:

    o The U.S. Department of State has discretion in deciding whether to vacate a Certificate of Loss of Nationality (CLN).
    o Unfortunately, the process lacks transparency, as specific rulings and reasons are not publicly available.

Remember that each case is unique, and seeking professional legal advice is crucial if you intend to restore your U.S. citizenship. It's essential to understand the implications fully before making any decisions.

Which country should I go to?

When someone renounces their U.S. citizenship, they typically choose another country to become a citizen of. Here are some common scenarios:

1. **Country of Residence:**

    o Many people who renounce U.S. citizenship already live abroad. They often choose the country where they

currently reside as their new citizenship.
- For example, if someone has been living in Canada, Australia, or the United Kingdom, they might opt for Canadian, Australian, or British citizenship.

2. Ancestral Ties:

- Some individuals explore their ancestral roots and choose a country based on family heritage.
- If someone has strong cultural or familial ties to a specific country, they might seek citizenship there.

3. Economic Citizenship Programs:

- Some countries offer citizenship by investment (also known as economic citizenship) programs.
- These programs allow individuals to acquire citizenship by making a significant investment in the country. Common investment options include real estate, government bonds, or other economic activities.
- Countries like Dominica, St. Kitts and Nevis, and Malta have popular

economic citizenship programs.

4. **Quality of Life and Lifestyle Preferences:**

   o People consider factors such as quality of life, healthcare, education, safety, and climate when choosing a new country.
   o Some prefer a slower pace of life, while others seek vibrant cities or natural beauty.

5. **Visa-Free Travel:**

   o Some individuals choose a country that offers visa-free or visa-on-arrival access to a wide range of other countries.
   o Having a passport from a visa-friendly country can simplify travel.

Remember that the choice of a new country depends on individual preferences, circumstances, and goals.

5 FINDING A NEW COUNTRY

While most countries allow dual citizenship and recognize former U.S. citizens as eligible for their citizenship, there are exceptions. Here are some relevant points:

1. **Countries That Allow Dual Citizenship**:
    - Many countries recognize dual citizenship, allowing individuals to hold more than one passport simultaneously.
    - Examples of countries that allow dual citizenship include Albania, Argentina, Australia, Canada, and the United Kingdom.

2. **Countries with Restrictions or Challenges**:
    - Some countries have limitations or specific requirements for former U.S. citizens seeking their citizenship.
    - However, outright refusal to accept former U.S. citizens as citizens is relatively rare.

3. **Countries with Historical Challenges**:
    - Historically, certain countries had stricter policies regarding dual citizenship or renunciation.
    - For instance, Algeria required renunciation of previous citizenship, but there was no specific prohibition on dual citizenship if acquired later.

4. **Research and Consultation**:
    - If you're considering obtaining citizenship in another country after renouncing U.S. citizenship, research the specific requirements and consult with legal experts.
    - Each country's laws and procedures vary, so seeking professional advice is crucial.

Remember that individual circumstances and country-specific rules play a significant role. Seeking legal advice and understanding the implications fully is essential.

6 REASONS TO RENOUNCE

People choose to renounce their U.S. citizenship for various reasons, and each case is unique. Here are some common motivations:

1. **Tax Considerations**:

    - **Double Taxation**: Some individuals renounce U.S. citizenship to avoid double taxation. The U.S. taxes its citizens on worldwide income, which can be burdensome for expatriates.
    - **Global Income Reporting**: U.S. citizens must report their global income, assets, and financial

accounts annually. Renouncing citizenship can simplify financial affairs and reporting requirements.

2. **Residency Abroad**:

   - Many expatriates renounce citizenship when they permanently reside in another country. They may feel more connected to their current country of residence.

3. **Political Beliefs or Disagreements**:

   - Some people renounce citizenship due to political reasons or disagreements with U.S. policies.
   - They may choose to express their dissent by relinquishing citizenship.

4. **Simplifying Financial Affairs**:

   - Renouncing citizenship can simplify estate planning, inheritance, and investments.
   - It allows individuals to focus on financial matters in their country of residence.

5. **Family Circumstances**:

    - Family ties, marriage, or cultural connections to another country may lead to renunciation.
    - Some individuals choose citizenship based on ancestral heritage.

6. **Quality of Life and Lifestyle Preferences**:

    - People seek a better quality of life, healthcare, education, or safety elsewhere.
    - Climate, culture, and lifestyle play a role in their decision.

Remember that renouncing U.S. citizenship is a significant step, and seeking professional advice is crucial.

7 EXCEPTIONS TO PAYING TAX

Let's dive into the intricacies of the exit tax (also known as the expatriation tax) when renouncing U.S. citizenship. While the exit tax can seem daunting, it's essential to understand that not every individual who renounces their U.S. citizenship will have to pay it. Here are some key points:

1. **Who Is Subject to the Exit Tax?**

    o The exit tax applies primarily to individuals categorized as "covered expatriates." These are people who

meet specific thresholds related to their net worth, taxable income, and tax compliance.
- If you do not fall under the covered expatriate definition, you will not be subject to the exit tax.

2. **Criteria for Covered Expatriates**: A covered expatriate is someone who meets any of the following criteria:

    - **Average Annual Net Income Tax Liability**: If your average annual net income tax liability for the five years preceding the expatriation year exceeds a specified threshold (adjusted for inflation, which was $178,000 for 2022).

    - **Net Worth**: If you have a net worth of $2 million or more on the expatriation date.

    - **Tax Compliance**: If you fail to certify, under penalties of perjury, compliance with all U.S. federal tax obligations for the five years preceding the expatriation year.

3. **Generous Exemption on Capital Gains**:

- Even if you are a covered expatriate, you may not owe exit tax thanks to the $767,000 exemption on capital gains.
- Consequently, many covered expatriates will not actually owe any exit tax due to this exemption.

4. **Types of Assets and Deemed Disposition**:
    - It's essential to consider your types of property and assets in relation to the exit tax.
    - Deemed dispositions of personal property and primary residences may be subject to capital gains tax, while certain financial accounts and interests in non-grantor trusts have special tax treatment.

5. **Understanding Deemed Disposition**:
    - A deemed disposition is a tax concept that treats certain assets as if they have been sold, even though no actual sale has occurred.
    - This notion is used in various tax jurisdictions to establish a taxable event, triggering the calculation of capital gains or losses for tax purposes.

Remember that the exit tax is not a punishment for renouncing citizenship; rather, it's a mechanism to ensure that individuals who have significantly benefited from their U.S. citizenship pay their fair share of taxes on their assets before leaving the U.S. tax system. If you have specific questions about your situation, consulting with a tax professional is advisable

Visit Arthurcrandon.co.uk for More Title

Retirement to the Philippines
K1 Fiance visa to the U.S. – Fast Track
Secrets to buying Condos in the Philippines
Buying Land in the Philippines
Annulment in the Philippines
Breaking free from a bad marriage
Get a visit visa to America First time
Marriage in the Philippines
Get a visit visa to the United Kingdom
Ghosts, Spectres, and folklore in the Philippines
Retiring to Spain – a Comprehensive Guide
Spousal Visa to America
Spousal visa to the United Kingdom
Working in the UK.
Working in the US.

ABOUT THE AUTHOR

Arthur Crandon is a retired lawyer and a prolific writer. He is British and grew up in a rural community in Somerset. He has lived in England, Wales, Hong Kong and the Philippines and now spends most of his time in the Philippines with his Visayan wife and their son.

He loves to hear from anyone who has anything to do with the Philippines – you can email him anytime on:

ac@arthurcrandon.co.uk

www.ingramcontent.com/pod-product-compliance
Lightning Source LLC
Chambersburg PA
CBHW070950220526
45471CB00007B/2968